Howard Andrew Millet Henderson

A Manual for Trustees and Teachers of Common Schools

Howard Andrew Millet Henderson

A Manual for Trustees and Teachers of Common Schools

ISBN/EAN: 9783337372910

Printed in Europe, USA, Canada, Australia, Japan

Cover: Foto ©Lupo / pixelio.de

More available books at **www.hansebooks.com**

A MANUAL

— FOR —

TRUSTEES AND TEACHERS

— OF —

COMMON SCHOOLS

Bound Copies, with Memorandum Pages attached, can be procured by addressing the Author, and enclosing 40 cts. The three Trustees and Teachers—4 copies—of any District, will be sent for 50 cts. post-paid.

———

SINGLE COPIES BY MAIL, - 25 cts.

.

PREFACE.

THIS little book is the product of the Autho. s
eight years experience, and will meet a need
for a simple guide to the legal performance of
the duties of District Officers. It details in simple
untechnical language, the laws as interpreted by
the Courts, the Attorney General and the State
Board of Education. All that this Manual contains
is based upon legal opinions, rendered by competent authority. To follow its prescriptions and
advice, is to escape all trouble. I have put it
forth from motives originating in a desire to give
Kentucky the benefit of my experience, and if
County Commissioners will put it in the hands of
every District Board, they escape a deal of annoy-
ance, and contribute toward the systematizing of
our Schools.

A MANUAL

—— FOR ——

TRUSTEES AND TEACHERS

Qualifications of a Trustee.

1. A Trustee must be a voter in the District, and must be a Justice of the Peace, or a teacher in the District of which he is a Trustee. He should be able to write, though it is not a *legal* necessity, but as in turn, he must become the Chairman, and must then post notices, make reports &c., the *reason of the case* implies sufficient knowledge to perform these duties without proxy·aids.

2. He must be a man of good moral character. That the law contemplates this is evident, from the fact that it requires this condition as a qualification for the Commissioner and for the teacher, and that a Commissioner has power to remove a Trustee for immorality.

3. He must be elected by the people at a legal election, or appointed, in case of a vacancy from any cause by the Commissioner, or hold over from the failure to elect a successor, or to qualify if elected.

4. He must be sworn in by the Commissioner, or by a Justice of the Peace, or some other officer designated by law to administer oaths. When sworn in by another officer than the Commissioner, a written statement to

that effect must be officially certified to the Commissioner.

5. A Trustee *in office* holds over until his successor is duly elected or qualified, or the Commissioner appoints.

6. A woman is not eligible to the office of Trustee.

Term of Office.

1. The first *legal* election under the new law (enacted in 1878), was held the 1st Saturday in June, 1879. The election held in June, 1878, was illegal, because the act was to take effect on the 1st day of June. The law requires ten days previous notice of an election, and of course, a legal notice, under this law could not have been given, as the act took effect on the same day the election was held—the 1st Saturday in June, 1878, having been the 1st day of June. The Trustees for the school year ending June 30th, 1879, held by the *appointment* of the Commissioner, their tenure of office being purely provisional, and their term expiring with the scholastic year. The three Trustees elected the 1st Saturday in June, 1879, constitute the *first* board under the new law, and they must cast lots to determine who shall serve one, two and three years. (Report for 1879, pages 129, 130, and 136)—each year hereafter but one Trustee will be elected, and he will serve three years—one going out each year. Where Districts failed to elect three Trustees, the Commissioner must fill the vacancies, and the Board when full, will proceed to organize as if all had been elected.

2. The term does not expire until June 30th, and the new Board can perform no official acts until the 1st day of July. Though sworn in before, it is contemplated that the oaths of office takes effect from the beginning of the school year.

Oath of Office.

1. The following form for the oath of office is prescribed by the State Board of Education :

" You do solemnly swear (or affirm) that you will support the Constitution of the United States and of the State of Kentucky, and that you will faithfully and impartially discharge the duties of Trustee of District No. ....., in the County of................., according to law, and the Rules and Regulations of the State Board of Education, and to the best of your ability."

2. When the oath is taken before a magistrate, or other officer than the Commissioner, the following is the form of certifying the fact to the Commissioner :

To the Common School Commissioner of...........County:

I certify that I did on the.........day of...............1879, administer the oath of office to A. B. a Trustee of District No. ......, of................County, and State of Kentucky.

Given under my hand and seal this......day of............. 187   C......... D.........,
                                   Justice of the Peace.

An oral statement or letter to the Commissioner from the Trustee is not sufficient.

3. The time appointed by the law for the Commissioner to adminster the oath of office is on the fourth Saturday in June. [Sec. 1, Chap. 193, Approved Feb. 20th, 1878.] It is desirable that every Trustee elect may present himself at the appointed time and place to the Commissioner, as it will avoid trouble in ascertaining who will accept the office, and it enables the Commissioner to give such counsel or instructions as he may desire. Trustees sworn in

8

by another should see that the Commissioner is officially notified of the fact. Trustees elect, designing not to accept the office, should notify the Commissioner, so that he may supply the vacancy by appointment.

At least one of the Trustees should be present to receive the blanks required for the use of the District, and carry them to the Chairman. By all being present at the time appointed. an organization can be at once effected, and the Commissioner notified as to who is the Chairman.

4. No act of a Trustee is legal until he is sworn. And, though a Trustee be sworn before. he cannot *act* until the first day of July subsequent to his election.

5. Trustees do not swear to reports. All is included under the original oath.

6. A Trustee re-elected need not again take the oath.

7. Any justice, notary public. or judge can administer the oath of office, but the Commissioner is not bound to recognize a Trustee unless he is officially notified of his having been qualified. In a general way it is better for the Commissioner to administer the oath to the Trustees.

8. Where there is a religious scruple against a judicial oath, the party will be allowed to affirm.

How to Organize.

1. Let the Trustees elect assemble at some place and time agreed upon. and decide by lot the length of the term of each. This may be done by the drawing of straws, the casting of dice, or by white cards, numbered from one to ten ; the person drawing the highest number

holding the long term, three years, the person drawing the next highest to serve the intermediate term (two years), and the person drawing the lowest number, the short term, (one year.)

2. The person having but one year to serve is Chairman of the Board.

3. When this matter is determined, the Chairman should call the Board to order, and proceed to business in systematic way, considering and concluding (if possible) one subject at a time.

4. As soon as the organization is effected, the Commissioner should be apprised in writing of the name and Post Office address of the Chairman.

5. Trustees, when they would transact business, must meet in regular session, and, *as a Board*, reach and *record* their conclusions. Of these meetings, all must have due and timely notice. The majority rules. Should the Chairman decline to execute the will of the Board, he may be reported to the Commissioner for removal, or compelled to do his duty by a *mandamus*.

The powers conferred by law upon the District Board must be exercised by the Board, meeting and deliberating at the same time and place, and not by one or two forming a determination and obtaining the assent of the absent. The decision of a majority at a meeting properly called is the decision of the Board, but the decision of a majority, or even of all three, under the other circumstances, is not the decision of the Board. It is merely the concurrent opinion of the members of the Board, and is no more the *decision* of the Board than the concurrent opinion of the members of the Legislature, arrived at by taking their separate votes at their respective homes, would be an act of the Legislature. The law supposes that a majority may be convinced by a minority and change its determination, and therefore will not allow the majority to act without giving the minority due notice to participate. This principle applies to the action of the Board in hiring a teacher, as well as to other matters.

It is held in 16 Maine R., 185, that the dismissal of a teacher by two, a majority of the Board, was illegal, because the third was not notified, although he was out of town. The Court say, " that does not allow the majority to dispense with the rule requiring notice. They are not in such cases constituted the judges whether the notice would be effectual to secure his attendance. Nor would it be entirely safe to intrust them with such a power, as it would afford an opportunity to select an occasion, when they might judge that a notice would be ineffectual, and thus, by neglecting to give it, free themselves from the presence of a dissenting minority. It may often happen that those will be able to attend, who were believed to be so situated that their attendance could not be expected. Nor is there any difficulty in giving the requisite notice in such cases, as one left at the usual place of residence would be sufficient."

6. *Board Record.*—"The law does not prescribe, nor has the State Superintendent directed, that any particular kind of record or account books shall be purchased. The Board should obtain such as are suited to the wants and means of the district. The contingent fund can be used to buy one. Every meeting should be recorded by a Secretary, and signed by him and the President.

7. It is the duty of the Chairman to execute contracts on the basis approved in a meeting of the Board before making. After being executed, it should be ratified in Board meeting and recorded.

8. The following are subjects of business :

1. To select books from the list recommended by the State Board, where the County Board has made no selection.

2. To select and contract with a teacher.

3. To make rules that do not contravene or conflict with those of the State Board.

4. To make a programme for the visitation of the school as required by law.

5. To levy the capulation tax of fifty cents upon the patrons for contingent expenses.

6. To provide fuel and necessary appendages for the School-house.

7. To consider the suspension or expulsion of an unruly pupil.

8. To decide upon the removal of the teacher in case of incompentency, and unacceptability, or immorality.

9. To make preparations for the building or repairing of the School-house, the calling out of the hands, the submission of the question of tax for that purpose *ad valorem* and *per capita*.*

10. To determine the question of submitting a vote for an *ad valorem* tax for any legal purpose, and to make the preliminary arrangements, if it is decided to submit.

11. To consider and make the legal reports required.

12. To make collection of District tax when voted.

Ad valorem means a tax upon the valuation of property. and *per capita* upon the heads of voters.

13. To consider any miscellaneous question affecting the interests of education in the District.

All these matters should be considered in a parliamentary way, the vote formally taken on every question, and every stage of the proceeding recorded and signed by the Chairman and Clerk. if there be one.

Liabilities of Trustees.

1. Trustees are liable, in their individual capacity, for the amount of money paid a Teacher who has no certificate, and for any contract that includes the payment of more money than the fund apportioned by the State, or realized from a District tax levied for paying the teacher will yield.

2. If Trustees contract with a Teacher for a less sum than that apportioned the District, and apply the remainder to other purposes, they are liable to an indictment for misdemeanor and can be sued for the recovery of said money. Let Trustees clearly comprehend that not a cent of the State money can, under any pretense, be expended for any other purpose than the payment of the teacher. Any balance, after paying the teacher, must be returned to the State Treasury and placed to the credit of the county in its surplus fund.

3. If Trustees dismiss a teacher for an illegal cause, they are liable to him under his contract. The dissatisfaction of patrons and pupils is no cause for the dismissal of a teacher. The *school* must be unsatisfactory. A teacher feeling aggrieved by the action of the Trustees in discharging him, may sue them for wages, or other damages, and thus compel them to show cause for the dismissal,

and to support their allegations by competent proof. The possession of a certificate is *prima facie* evidence of the teacher's competency, and hence, when the Trustees discharge a teacher, they assume the burthen of proof as to the alleged grounds of his incompetency. The cause or causes assigned for dismissal in the written notices thereof is conclusive, and estops from showing any other or different causes.--[Paul *vs.* School District in Hartland, 23 Vt., 575, and Neville *vs.* Directors of District No. 1, 36 Ill., 31,]

4. A failure or refusal of the Trustees to make the reports required of them, within the specified time, subjects them to a fine of not less than twenty dollars, and an action for damages by any person injured thereby —[Sec. 9, Art. II, Chap. 18, Gen. Stats.]

5. The failure of a Trustee resigning, within ten days thereafter, to deliver to his successor, any money, property, books or papers in his custody as Trustee, subjects him to a fine of twenty dollars, and it is made the duty of the Commissioner to report any such delinquency to the Grand Jury. - [Sec. 18, Art. V, Chap xviii, Gen. Stats.]

5. For any neglect of duty or malfeasance in office, in addition to the paying fine, he shall be removed from office by the Commissioner.—[Sec. 19, Art. VI, Chap. xviii, Gen. Stats.]

6. A failure to enforce the rules and regulations of the State Board of Education, to monthly visit the school, to provide fuel, &c., for the school-house, are instances of neglect of duty justifying removal.

7. Employing a teacher without a certificate, allowing more than one text-book on the same subject to pupils of

the same grade to be taught, making a false census report, and appropriation of any portion of the public money to other uses than the payment of the teacher, are instances of misfeasance.

8. A representation that a teacher having a certificate cannot be obtained to teach the school, with the view of obtaining a license for a favorite to teach, is an offense. A license is only to be granted as a last resort. It is not the privilege of the Trustees, but an expedient in an emergency, and must be so recognized by the Commissioner, and a license refused when a qualified teacher can be obtained.

9. Should a teacher be removed by the Trustees, they are liable for his pay for the time he taught. The balance due the District may be paid his successor.

10. When a Commissioner has legally condemned a school-house, and notified the Trustees thereof, and they fail to take the necessary steps to repair or build, a writ of *mandamus* will lie to the Trustees, commanding and compelling them to discharge their duty, and any citizen interested may sue out said writ.—[Beverly *vs.* Sabin, 20 Ill., and Cotton *vs.* Reed, Ibid, 607.]

11. Should Trustees willfully make a false census list, besides being liable to an indictment for perjury, he is subject to a fine of not less than twenty dollars.—[Sec. 14, Art. VII, Chap. 18, Gen. Stats.]

12. Should Trustees contract with a teacher to pay him the sum apportioned the District, and afterwards consent under Sec. 5, Art. VI to the transfer of a pupil to another district, they make themselves responsible for the sum thus alienated from the teacher of their own District.

13. The Trustees are liable if they fail to make settlement with the Commissioner for the local tax money paid out upon their order, and should the Commissioner detect any fraud or misappropriation of funds, they can be proceeded againt by the Commissioner.—[Sec. 6, Art. II, Chap, xviii, Gen. Stats.]

14. Should Trustees permit more than one book for pupils of the same grade to be used in the school, the fund apportioned the District may be withheld; and if they require a teacher to violate this rule of the State Board of Education, they are liable for the amount to the teacher, if the Commissioner should withhold the School Fund.—[See Rules and Regulations of State Board, Sec. 19.]

15. Any Trustee or Trustees who shall knowingly and willfully misreport, under oath, any fact or facts now or hereafter required of them to be reported, shall be deemed guilty of false swearing, and *shall be punished by confinement in the Penitentiary not less than one, nor more than five years.*—[See Art. VIII, Chap xxvii, Gen. Stats.]

This appalling statute should make Trustees scrupulously exact in making their reports, and not to employ a cent of the fund derived, from the State, for any other purpose than the payment of the teacher.

16. Trustees who fail, after the school-house has been condemned by the Commissioner, to have a good and sufficient school-house in their District within six months thereafter, shall be liable to be indicted by a grand jury and fined, as overseers of the highway are fined, for failing to keep their precinct road in good repair, unless the Commissioner gives farther time, which cannot be ex-

tended beyond six months.—[Sec. 8, Art. VII, Chap. xviii, Gen. Stats.]

17. For a failure of a Chairman of a Board of Trustees to report a school for payment when half and when wholly taught out, and at the close ot the year to make his annual report, he is subject to a fine of not less than twenty dollars, and is liable to action for damages by any aggrieved person.—[Sec. 16, Art. VII, Chap. xviii, Gen. Stats.]

The Posting of Notices for the Election of Trustees.

1. The Chairman of the Board in office must post notices at three or more prominent places in the District ten days* betore the election, that an election for a Trustee will be held at such time and place. Printed notices are furnished each Chairman by the Commissioner.

2. In reckoning the length of time required for posting this notice of an election,, either the day on which the notice was posted, or the day on which the election is held will be counted.

3. The Chairman is the sole judge of the three most prominent places. His object should be to give the widest possible notice to the voters of the District.

The District Tax.

1. In the submission of the question of tax, the Trustees of a Country District cannot submit more than 25 cents on each $100 worth of property, but can any amount less.

---

* Notices for the Tax must be posted fifteen days before an election.

2. A Town or City can, under the General Statutes, submit a *maximum* tax of 30 cents on the $100 worth of property.

3. The Chairman of a Board of Trustees must post the notices at three or more prominent places in the District, and fifteen days in advance of the vote. The notices must clearly state the object or objects for which it is proposed to levy the tax. It is not sufficient to state the gross amount, without detailing the *purposes* to which it is proposed to apply it. The notices must be signed by the Commissioner and the Chairman of the Board of Trustees. Fifteen days' notice must include the day the notices are posted. If the day the vote is taken is counted, *it* would be the sixteenth day.

4. The purposes for which a tax is submitted must be for:

(1.) The purchase of the site or the building or repairing of a school-house.

(2.) The better payment of the teacher, or for extending the legal term beyond five or three months, as the number of pupil children may require.

(3.) The furnishing of the house with desks, or seats or black-boards, maps, charts, etc. If more than one purpose is included in the notice, *each* design must be named ; for instance : Suppose the gross amount is 20 cents, to be distributed between school objects, each must be named, as follows: (1.) Ten cents for purchasing a site and building a house ; (2.) Five cents for furnishing the house ; (3.) Five cents for the better payment of the teacher, or to secure his services for a longer time than the legal term.

5. The tax can be voted for from one to five years, but the *time* must be stated.

6. The question may be submitted as many times during the school year as that fifteen days' previous notice can be given. Trustees are, however, *advised* not to submit it more than twice in one year.

7. Trustees may anticipate the whole amount to be realized, and contract on that basis, and should be careful in making their estimates not to exceed the gross amount it will yield for the term for which it is voted, if they would not make themselves liable for a deficiency.

8. The Officers should remember that the District can not be changed in any respect during the time for an *ad-valorem* tax, which is levied.

9. " White qualified voter " is one who has resided in the State two years, and in the County one year, and in the Precinct in which the District is included, in whole or in part, sixty days, next preceding the election.

See Gen'l Stats.. Art. 2, Sec. 8, and Art. 3, Secs. 8 and 9 of Chapter 33; and "Kentucky School Lawyer," pages 36-38.

This general rule will apply to the case. Anything that would permit a man to vote at any other election, will permit him to vote at a school election.

The exceptions are :

(1.) A widow having children between six and twenty years of age, may vote in person or by written proxy,

(2.) A widow who is a tax payer.

(3.) An alien or unnaturalized foreigner within the census of, or who is a tax payer, in the District. Non-residents, though tax-payers, can not vote.

10. Trustees may choose to collect the tax of the owner

or of a tenant, if his contract with the proprietor is to pay the taxes, whichever they may deem most eligible. The property is bound for the taxes, and may be distrained by the Trustees, or the Collector commissioned, by them the same as a Sheriff can distrain for the collection of State or County taxes.

A vote of a District is binding on the tax payers, after the Trustees have made a contract based upon it.

All moneys loaned out of the District, and bonds subject to taxation for other purposes, are taxable in the District where the lender or owner resides.

11. "A fair and true record of the votes," taken for or against the tax, must be returned by the Officers of the Election to the Commissioner, certified and sworn to by them. If the Commissioner has presided at the election, returns must be made to the County Judge.

12. It is the duty of the Commissioner to furnish whoever is appointed to collect the tax, with the boundary of the District, certified officially by him. *Sec. 3, Art II, Gen'l Stats.*

13. When furnished by the Commissioner with the boundary, the Collector will ascertain from the Assessor's books what property is subject to taxation, and this must be his guide in making the levy for collection.

14. "A fair and true record" is one kept in a poll-book and numbered (1, 2, 3, etc.), the votes summed up at the bottom of each page, certified over the signatures of the officers of the election, sworn to before a proper officer, with the names of the Judge and Clerk at the foot of each page, signed as filled, so that the same may be identified.

15. Whoever is charged with the collection must collect

and pay over the tax within two months, to the Commissioner, unless otherwise directed by the Board of Trustees, and he and his sureties are liable to the Board, the same as a Sheriff is for State and County taxes.—*Sec. 8, Art. 8, Chap. 92, General Statutes.*

16. The order of the Trustees for the payment of the money must be honored by the Commissioner, and this order, *in writing*, is his sufficient voucher.

17. Should a Trustee use this money, or order it to be used, contrary to the purpose contemplated by the law, he is liable to an indictment for a misdemeanor.

18. Trustees should apply money to the payment of a competent Teacher for the legal term, rather than to secure longer service by an indifferent instructor. The best economy is to have well done what is done. The quality rather than the quantity of instruction should be the standard of judgment, when devoting the proceeds of the local tax to the payment of a teacher.

19. The Trustees are required to make settlement with the Commissioner, of all moneys derived from District taxation, disbursed upon their order, by exhibiting receipts from the parties to whom the money has been paid, and they are, for a failure to do so, liable to a fine of twenty dollars, and to an action for damages instituted by any person injured thereby.—*Secs. 15 16, Art. 7.*

This settlement should be made with the Commissioner on or before the termination of each school year.

20. The Trustees of any city or town, having a special charter authorizing a less tax than 30 cents in the $100 of property, may, under Sec. 9, Art. 2 of Chap. 19, General Statutes, levy an amount not exceeding 30 cents.

21. Cities or towns may, under Sec. 9 of Art. 11, establish a system of graded schools. The method of procedure in such cases is prescribed in Sec. 5, Art. 6 of Chap. 18, General Statutes, which consult, with notes in " The School Lawyer," pages 131 and 132, and Superintendent's Annual Report for the year ending June 30th, 1879, page 142.

Cautions to Trustees About to Assess or Collect a Tax.

1. Follow the prescription of the law to the letter. An irregularity which would not void an election for Trustees will defeat an election for the levy of a tax.

2. It is important that the notices of the election should be legally given, and the evidence of the notices should be preserved.

3. Meet, *as a Board*, resolve to submit the question of tax on a *definite* day ; determine for how many *amounts* on the $100 worth of property you will take the vote : divide into cents the amount to be raised, and so express it in the notices, that is, say how many cents to the $100 you propose for *each object* for which you propose to raise the tax.

4. Make your action a matter of record ; select the places where you will post the notices, and the Trustee who will do it, make them out at the time, and get the Commissioner's and Chairman's signatures, select the three most prominent places in the District, and let the object be to apprize every voter of the proposed election; put the notices up so that *fifteen* days will transpire before the day of the election.

5. If there is any question about the boundaries of the District, have them accurately described, in writing, by the Commissioner before assessing the tax-payers. Have the officers you wish to hold the election engaged, and be at the place with you at the proper time prepared to organize for an election.

6. As soon as the election is successful get the tax list from the assessor's books and make out a tax-bill for each tax-payer, in form as follows :

Form of Tax Bill.

Assessment of the Taxes upon the ratable estate of ....in District No...............of the County of.......................State of Kentucky, made by the Trustees thereof, according to law, this................... day of.......................18......for the purpose of (here state the object), *according to a vote of said District, held on...............day of.......................18......*

Names.	Real.	Personal.	Total.	Tax.

The Chairman should sign the Tax Bill. This Bill is not necessary. A list given the Collector is sufficient to meet the law, but this plan will be best.

7. The Trustees may collect themselves or appoint the

Collector. If the Board appoint they need not, but may require bond, and if they do they should fix the sum and approve the sureities. They should agree with the Collector for his fees, or he will be entitled to ten per cent.

Collector's Bond.

Know all men, that we, A B, of .... State of Kentucky, as principal, and C D, of .... as surety, are firmly held and bound unto Trustees of school district No. .... in the county of ...., and state aforesaid, in the full sum of [to be fixed by the District, not exceeding double the tax] to be paid to the said Trustees their successors in said office, or assigns, to which we jointly bind ourselves, our several and respective heirs, executors and administrators.

Sealed and dated this .... day of .........A.D. 18......

The condition of this obligation is, that whereas the said A B was, at a meeting of the Board and Trustees of school District No. ...... of the connty of .... appointed a collector of the rates and taxes assessed and to be assesssd in, by and upon said district, and the said A B has accepted said office ; and whereas said District on the .... day of .... A. D 18...... voted that a tax has been legally assessed, and the Trustees of said District hath issued their warrant to said Collector, with said rate bill annexed, for the collection of said tax, the receipt of which said rate bill and warrant is hereby acknowledged, and by which said warrant, said tax is collected and paid over, on or before the .... day of .... A.D. 18.. ... Now if the said A B shall faithfully perform and discharge said office and trust, and with dilligence and

fidelity, levy and collect, as far as may be done, all the
taxes that have been, or may be so committed to him for
collection, during his continuance in office, and he, his
heirs, executors or administrators shall, at all times on
proper demand, render an account and pay over all the
proceeds of such collections to the Commissioner of said
County, or the successor in office, according to the direc-
tions contained in the warrants for their collection, then
this obligation is to be void, otherwise to remain in force.

Executed in presence of   [L. S.]

        [L. S.]

Warrant to Collect a Tax.

*To A B, collector of taxes of School District No......of the
County of ...... and State of Kentucky:*—GREETING.

You, having been appointed Collector of taxes for said
District, are hereby, in the name of said State, authorized
and required to proceed and collect the tax specified in
the annexed rate bill, according to law, and to pay the
same to the Commissioner of the County, or to his successor in office; and for so doing this shall be your
sufficient warrant.

Given under my hand and seal, at ...... this ...... day of
.... A.D. 18......

        C. D.   [L. S.]

Chairman of the Board of Trustees of said School
District.

Construction as to Tax.

1. If the homestead be in a District voting a tax, all
the lands *attached* to it are subject to taxation in that
District and no other.

2. The property of a manufacturing Company in a tax-voting District is subject to the levy.

3. The property of non residents must be taxed.

4. An omission, through error, to assess one does not invalidate the tax as against others. (21 Pick., 76 ; 6 Mit., 498.)

5. The tax may be voted for five years, and the proceeds, in contracting, be anticipated by the Trustees.

6. No change can be made in the boundary of any District while it is subject to a local levy, voted by the electors thereof.

7. When parties plead they live out of the District, or have no pupil children, and, therefor, can not be benefitted by the tax. let the Trustees reply that the Common Schools are conducted for the good of the State, and not to confer a private benefit. Men have to work the roads who do not own a wheel or beast. All members of society are interested in good citizenship, and property-holders most of all.

8. The Trustees must be careful to expend every cent in accordance with the notice, and all action directing expenditures shall be made in Board Meeting and recorded. If it be to build a School-house define and record the location. secure the deed before beginning work, and the plan of the building or its repairs.

9. The Collector must pay over the District tax within two months unless otherwise directed by the Justices, or he will render his sureties liable, and the Trustees should take the precaution to so inform him. He has all the power of distraint the Sheriff has in collecting the State Taxes.

The Chairman should give all orders upon the amount for money in writing.

Make settlement with the Commissioner at the close of each *school* year (30th of June), and get a *quietus*, which file.

NOTE—For anything farther as to what property is subject to taxation and exemption, see " School Lawyer " pp. 43, 48.

How to Organize for and Conduct an Election.

1. The Chairman should be at the voting place promptly at the hour, namely,* one o'clock, with the poll book furnished by the Commissioner, and call the electors present to order, saying : " Citizens, we have come together for the purpose of electing a Trustee of School District No............, and of determining whether a tax of..............cents on the hundred dollars shall be levied for common school purposes.' State the purpose to which it is proposed to apply the tax. Ask, " Who will you have for Judge ?" When the nominations are concluded, take the vote in the order in which the candidates were named, by saying. " Those of you in favor of E. F. for Judge will hold up your right hands." Count them and proceed until it is known who the electors have chosen. In like manner proceed to elect a clerk.

2. If there be no one present at the appointed time, the Chairman will wait until some one comes. As soon as one man comes, let the Chairman designate him as Judge, act as clerk himself, and let the election proceed.

3. The law does not prescribe that the Judge and clerk shall take an oath. The law is satisfied when they prop-

* If to vote a tax, the State Board has decided that the vote must be taken between 9 A. M. and 5 P. M.

erly certify to the Commissioner the returns and who is elected, and whether or not the tax was voted.

4. As soon as the officers of the election are determined, let the Chairman give to the clerk the poll-book, and let the voting begin.

5. The judge of a district election must, within five days after an election, cause the poll-book of said election to be placed in the hands of the County Commissioner. It must be added up, and a certificate thereon must show that a certain person has been elected. This must be certified by the Judge and Clerk. The record of a case, from Marion county, showed that the report was not added up, and no one was certified by name as elected, and the poll-book was not certified. The Commissioner refused to receive it as official and appointed Trustees. It was decided that it was not the business of the Commissioner to add up the poll and determine the result. That no one was certified as elected. That he had no official testimony that the poll was the poll of the district, as the voters were registered in pencil, and the figure 1, 1, 1, &c., placed opposite each elector's name. The record should have been in ink, and the votes registered in cumulative figures—1, 2, 3, &c.—and should have contained a certificate showing who was elected, signed by the officers of the election. The Commissioner was sustained.

It was decided *obiter dicta* that the Trustees qualified could only be removed by a *writ quo warranto* in a civil court, the State Board having no jurisdiction over *writs*. It was said that the parties could have (1) enjoined the Commissioner from qualifying the appointed Trustees until the matter of the appeal was decided by the Board ;

or (2), they could by a *mandamus*, if one could be obtained, try the question—the writ sued for, to direct the Commissioner to recognize the parties claiming to have been elected. That these steps not having been taken, the Trustees in office could only be removed by a *quo warranto*. When officers have been recognized and qualified by a Commissioner, the remedy for parties claiming an election is not before the State Board, but in a civil court, having the power to subpœna witnesses.

For the benefit of Trustees not versed in the terms of the law, we define—

(1.) An *injunction* is a judicial writ or process requiring a party to do or refrain from doing a particular thing. If parties claiming to be elected Trustees have reason to believe that, pending an appeal, the Commissioner proposes to qualify other parties, they may enjoin him from so doing. But the Commissioner has the right, pending the appeal or contest, to recognize whomsoever he will until the appeal or contest has been determined.

(2.) A *mandamus* is a writ issued from a court of competent jurisdiction, directing a person to do some specified thing, as in the case of Trustees to require the Commissioner to qualify certain persons claiming to have been elected Trustees.

(4.) A *quo warranto* is a writ against certain parties, requiring them to show by what authority they hold their claim; as in the case of Trustees qualified by a Commissioner to show by what authority they were introduced to office.

(4.) A *contest* controverts the claims of other parties, and sets up what is supposed to be a superior claim.

6. Votes cannot be recorded before or after the hour

appointed for an election ; but shonld the officers be tardy in opening the election, and voters should wait and vote, so that no one was deprived of his right to vote,* the election would not be invalidated. The Trustees should always be present at the appointed hour, and organize for the election, among themselves, if other patrons are not present.

7. The certificate of the officers of a district election is the legal evidence of a Trustee's election ; and a Commissioner is justifiable in refusing to recognize a person claiming the Trustee's office until he brings a certificate of election.

8. Elections for tax may be held any time during the year, after fifteen days' notice has been given.

9. A Judge of an election, if a voter of the District, has one vote as an elector, and another as Judge in case of a tie.

9. Statutory residence as a voter in a precinct, which includes a district or a part thereof, entitles a patron to vote in a school election when changed from one district to another in the same precinct, or a part thereof.

10. Voters are required to possess the qualifications of electors at a general election, and no others. The exceptions are in the cases of widows and aliens.

NOTE.—For other information concerning who may vote, see "Kentucky School Lawyer," pages 36-38. Constitution, Sec. 8, Art. II.

District Boundaries.

1. Boundaries should always be recorded in the Commissioner's book, described by geographical land-marks,

---

* If it could be shown that by this delay voters were deprived of their votes, and that had these been taken, the result would have been changed, it would invalidate the election.

and not by the name of patrons. A copy should be furnished the Trustees of each district.

2. Several cases came up in Bourbon involving changes of boundary. In one instance a new district had been made by taking territory from two others. It was alleged that the Commissioner had failed to give the written notice required by Section 1 of Article 6, Chapter 18, General Statutes. He appeared and gave affidavit that he had given written notice. It was decided that, in this case, there could be discovered by the Board no improper motive in making the changes ; that the majority were adverse to his action, and included Justices of the Peace upon whose favor he relied for re-election, and that he was of unimpeachable character, and could not have forgotten a matter of so much official importance ; and, as the appellants did not pretend to impeach his veracity, and these statements were a matter of memory, and the act of the Commissioner, presumptively, a matter of record, the Board sustained his action, believing it to have been prompted by a conviction that the creation of the new districts was for the good of the Common Schools in his county.

3. A case was appealed on the ground that the Commissioner had not given written notice. The record showed that all the parties interested in the change were present and entered their objections. It was decided that the voluntary appearance of the parties was a waiving of notice—the purpose of the law having been met by their voluntary presence. The Commissioner was, therefore, sustained.

4. A boundary cannot be changed while a tax-levy, voted by the electors, remains in force.

5. A change of boundary must be made before the

taking of the census, and a written notice given the Trustees of each district to be affected thereby of the time and place to hear objections. After hearing objections, the Commissioner has the right to make the change, except as set forth in 4.

6. The boundary of a fractional district cannot be changed except by the mutual consent of the Commissioners of the two counties, or upon appeal to the State Board. The site of the school-house determines the question of county jurisdiction. In whatever county the house is situated. to that county the jurisdiction belongs.

7. No Board of Trustees should fail to require of the Commissioner a written boundary description.

Census.

1. It is the duty of the Board of Trustees, during the month of April, to *take* the census. If they *have it taken* they must pay for it themselves. If not done by them by the 10th of May, the Commissioner can have it done and pay for it with money deducted from the apportionment by the State to the district.—*Sec. 7, Art VII., Chap. 18. G. S.*

If done by neither, the Superintendent will take the census of the previous year as the basis of apportionment. —*Sec. 7, Art. I., Ohap. 18, G. S.*

2. It is the duty of the Chairman to make his Census Report before the 10th of May. The Commissioner has to report to the Superintendent by the 1st of June.—*Sec. 7, Art. V., Chap. 18, G. S.*

3. The school age includes *all* children between six and twenty years of age, even if married.

4. Children of people moving into a district before the

census is taken, but not having acquired citizenship, can be embraced in the census. If they come from another state after the census is taken, and send pupils to school, the teacher has the right to charge them tuition. If they are citizens of Kentucky, they can send to the school, though enrolled elsewhere.

5. Pupils omitted by the census-taker are not barred the school, though no money can be drawn for them. When the apportionment tables are once made up, the Superintendent has no fund left with which to pay for children left out by the officers.

6. If the mistake is the Trustees', the Board is responsible ; if the Commissioner's, he is liable for the amount they would have drawn had they been reported at the proper time to the Superintendent.

7. The Trustees should be put in possession, by the Commissioner, of the written boundary of the district, geographically described, and not by the names of heads of families. Trustees must be careful not to report children belonging to another district, as the law prescribes a heavy penalty.—*Sec. 6, Art. VIII., Chap. 27, G. S.* The Commissioner should compare the Census Reports and see that children are not reported more than once, and only where they belong. Done willfully, it is a penitentiary offence.

8. The residence of a child is that of its parent, guardian, or master (if an apprentice). If a child were a citizen, and had the right to vote in the district, it would have the right to attend school. Children cannot be sent to relatives or friends with a view of being sent to the District School *free of charge.* A property-holder living

in another district cannot send his children (free) to a school in which he pays school-tax.

9. A child must be six years old on or before the 1st day of July, and less than twenty by one day, at least, on the 1st day of July, to be reported in the census. Proper questions to ask :

(1.) How many children have you, who will be six years old on the 1st day of July, and less than twenty years old on the 30th day of June ?

(2.) What is your name (parent, guardian, or master) in full ?

(3.) What are the Christian names of your girls ? Boys ?

(4.) Have you given your children to a census-taker this year ?

10. Cities, reporting directly to the Superintendent, may be required to send him the detailed report—the same as that the Trustees deliver to the Commissioner. It must contain the names of parents or guardians, the names of pupils, the street, number of residence, and age of each pupil.

11. When cities do not report in time, it is in the power of the Superintendent to employ a person to take the census, and deduct the cost of the same from the fund apportioned the district.

12. Children in any of the State Schools cannot be reported, as they are already enjoying the benefits of education at public cost. These institutions are :

(1.) The Agricultural and Mechanical College.
(2.) The Institution for Deaf and Dumb.
(3.) The Institution for the Blind.
(4.) The Institution for Feeble-minded Children.

13. A child that will be six years of age on the 1st day of July cannot be reported. Persons who will be twenty on that day cannot be reported. The census taken in April is for the scholastic year beginning July 1st.

14. Residence is not acquired by *temporary* removal to a district for the purpose of sending children to school.

15. A Commissioner changed a boundary, and failed to make the change a matter of record. Afterward it was sought to invalidate an election by throwing out the votes of the electors living without the district as described by the record, but within as it was orally changed by the Commissioner. The census report had included the parties objected to, and it was proved that for several years they had exercised the rights and paid the costs of patrons. It was decided, that the electors could not be made to suffer on account of the *laches* of the Commissioner. The census and poll-books for several years were introduced by the parties, and were received as testimony. The election was validated, and the Commissioner ordered to amend his official record.

16. The consent of the Trustees of adjoining districts (*Sec. 5, Art. VI., Chap. 18, G. S.*) for a pupil to go to school out of the district, and to pay the teacher thereof, does not change the *census* relation of the pupil to the district giving consent. If a contract is made with a teacher for the public money apportioned the district, and the Trustees consent to the transfer of a pupil and its *per capita*, the teacher can claim of the Trustees. If done, he must assent to relinquish his claim.

Certificates.

1. Teachers must have a certificate or license to be

competent to contract for a school. He must have a cerificate or license to render valid every day of teac hing.

2. A County certificate permits a teacher to teach in any District in his County.

3. A State certificate enables him to teach in any District in the State. .

4. A license is only good for a specified school and term. Trustees should never employ a teacher on a license, when one can be obtained possessing a certificate. Commissioners should never issue a license when a teacher with a certificate can be secured. Its a great mistake to suppose that anybody that can read is fit to teach little children. The *best* teachers ought to teach beginners.

5. A Commissioner can, for legal reason, revoke a teacher's certificate. A revocation annuls the contract. In such a case the teacher must be paid for the time he taught *with a certificate.* If his certificate has been revoked without legal causes, his redress is in the Commissioner.

6. If a Board of Trustees dismiss the teacher without legal reason, they are responsible, and the teacher may recover from them.

7. Certificates are of the following classes and grades:

(1.) A first grade 1st class certificate.

(2.) A second grade, 1st class certificate.

(3.) A second class certificate. There are *first and second grade.* Second class certificates.

(4.) A license.

(5.) A State certificate good anywhere.

(6.) Certificates issued by City Boards, and good only for the schools controled by them.

8. Whoever contracts to teach a Common School must

have a certificate, and whoever does the actual teaching.
A person without a certificate, though a master of arts,
and a President of a University is not competent to contract without a certificate. By "qualified teacher" the
law means one having a County, State, or City certificate,
good only where issued. ·License *ought* to mean nothing
but *lie-sense.* Better *no* school than one taught by a sham
and shift who cannot get the lowest grade certificate.

9. A teacher failing to attend the Institute, unexcused
by the Commissioner for *good* reasons, forfeits his certificate, and every day he teaches thereafter is *illegal*, and he
is not entitled to pay.

10. Should a teacher be degraded, and on appeal have
his certificate restored, he can claim pay—for such loss,
in such a case, is not his act, but that of the agents of the
State. He has, also, the right of action against those
parties to the transaction, for damages, if any have re-
sulted.

Who Employs the Teacher and Contracts With Him.

1. The Board of Trustees, having supervision during
the term the school is taught, is alone competent to employ the teacher, and a majority of the Board must
concur in his employment. An old Board cannot employ a teacher, even though two holding over agree
thereto. ·It must wait until the new member is qualified.
The Board must act together in regular session in the
transaction of *all* its business. . .Each member must be
notified by the Chairman of the time and place of meeting.
A Chairman is not competent to contract without the

concurrence of one of the other members of the Board.

2. When an Assistant Trustee is needed, the Trustees have the right to employ him, as he is responsible to the Board for his share of the conduct of the school.

3. A contract made with a teacher before the Board is qualified and organized, and with a teacher who has no certificate at the time of contracting, is not a legal contract.

4. The form of agreement with a teacher is printed in the Teachers' Register, furnished each District. Contracts should always be in writing, and signed by all the contracting parties.

5. The contract should state who is to attend to the school-house, furnishing fuel, &c.

6. A contract can not be enforced by law, which contemplates a longer term, *for the public* money than the legal term of three or five months. The amount apportioned the District is the salary *the State* pays its officer for a definite service as to quantity, quality and duration.

7. No contract contemplating the use of a part of this salary for ulterior purposes can be enforced.

8. Trustees should contract with the teacher for a definite amount. If they exceed the public money or the amount supplemented by the local tax, or a reliable subscription, Trustees render themselves liable for the deficiency. It is competent to contract for the apportionment without designating the amount. Whatever is hypothecated without conditions, the Board is obligated to pay, and should the anticipated revenues not be realized, they are responsible to the teacher in his individual capacity, unless otherwise expressly stipulated.

9. No more service can be required of a teacher *for the*

public money apportioned the District than the law, and regulations governing Common Schools require. A failure of a teacher to comply with extra requirements, involving time, talent and labor, would not invalidate the contract, but he could claim the apportionment if he could show that he had done all the State required of him. Trustees are the agents and officers of the State to secure a specific and stated result, and they have no right to speculate upon the teacher's (also an officer of the State) necessities, to extort more from him than his employer—the State, requires of him.

10. Trustees bind themselves, individually and collectively, when they promise more than the State agrees to pay. They should, hence, contract for the public fund without anticipating a definite amount.

11. Trustees act for the District in contracting on the basis of the local tax, and this is a matter purely conventional, between them and the teacher.

12. Contracts, to be legally binding, must be made by the Board in its corporate capacity. Though its members are qualified before, the Board can not organize for business until the 1st day of July. Though two members remain they can not contract until the junior member is legally in office—the 1st day of July. Any contract made before is void *ab initio* (from the beginning.)

13. The Trusteees have no right to grant holidays not granted by the State.

14. If the teacher chooses to teach on holidays he can, and count the time. He may not teach Saturday, without special agreement. By mutual consent only can the school be adjourned for the statutory holidays occurring during the term.

15. The teacher does not lose time because of freshets, epidemics &c. He does when he himself is not at the school-house, no matter what the cause. Should he be locked out and go to the house he can count the time. He can not force an entry as against the Trustees, but may count the time.

16. Should the Trustees, when responsible under the contract, fail to furnish fuel in cold weather, and the pupils shonld leave in consequence thereof, the teacher may, also, do so, even though he send the children home. He must be able to prove, however, that it would have been cruel, and impaired health to have detained them. He can not make the pupils do menial service. It must be voluntary whenever rendered. If the teacher has made himself responsible by agreement, for the comfort of the pupils, and fails to provide the conditions thereto, he looses the time.

17. Oral contracts must be clearly prove l, or the presumptions of the case will interpret, and locate responsibility.

18. Should a house be destroyed by fire or flood, or tempest, or mob-violence, the teacher does not lose the time.

School Term.

1. A District containing forty pupils and more. must have a school of five months, or one hundred and ten days.

1. A District containing thirty-nine pupils and less, must be taught three months, or sixty-six days.

3. A District School in which there is an average

attendance of sixty or more pupils must have an assistant teacher, who must have a certificate.

4. A school term must be included within the school year, and must be continuous.

Holidays.

1. The only legal Holidays are the twenty-second of February, the Fourth of July, Christmas day (not week), and days of Thanksgiving and Fast proclaimed by the Governor. If either of these days occur during the school term, the Trustee *may* count them, provided he *agrees* with the teacher to this effect, and not otherwise.

2. The teacher is entitled to count the time he is in actual attendance upon the County Institute, *provided*, the Institute occurs during the school term, and not otherwise. The Trustee cannot subtract this time, as the teacher forfeits his certificate should he fail to attend.

3. A school cannot be dismissed on account of an epidemic, or cold weather, or a freshet, except by the mutual consent of the Trustees and teacher. If the teacher consents he loses the time.

4. Should a storm or fire render the school-house untenantable, the Trustee must immediately procure another house. The teacher does not lose the time when suspension ensues from the act of God.

5. The school cannot be suspended for a meeting of any kind.

6. By "school days" are meant all days, except Saturday and Sunday, legal holidays, and while the teacher is in attendance upon the Institute.

Incompatible Offices.

1. A Trustee cannot be a Justice of the Peace, or a County Judge, or a Common School teacher.

2. A teacher cannot be a Trustee, or an Overseer of the Road.

3. A teacher may hold the office of Commissioner, but must arrange his school so that he can visit each district *school.* Should he fail to visit the *school,* he is not entitled to the three dollars pay, apportioned for this work. It is not sufficient that he visits the District.

Exemptions.

1. A Chairman of the Board of Trustees is exempt from *all* jury service, militia duty, and work upon the highway. Other Trustees are not exempt from these services.

2. A teacher is not exempt from such services. When called upon to work the road he must serve, or pay the penalty. If he works, he loses the time.

Contingent Fee.

1. The Trustees have the right to exact fifty cents from each patron (a person actually sending children to school) to supply fuel, brooms, and to pay for taking care of the school-room. If the teacher does this, the money may be paid him, if so agreed.

2. When this money is not required for the necessaries of the school-house (such as fuel, buckets, brooms, etc.), the poll-tax may be levied and collected, and the money applied to furnishing the school-room, or purchasing a blackboard, maps, charts, globes, dictionary, record book, Guide to Trustees, etc.

3. The Trustees may *warrant* delinquent patrons, but cannot distrain.

4. It is not a teacher's duty to make fires, provide fuel, sweep the floor, etc. The contract should never fail to clearly express by whom these things are to be provided, and who is to perform this service. If a teacher voluntarily assumes this service, he may be held to his contract, and should he fail to perform his self-assumed duties it would be ground for annulling the contract.

5. The Trustees may assess only so much as may be necessary to pay costs, and may accept its equivalent in wood, or needed articles, or necessary labor (such as cutting wood, digging a well, etc.)

6. The tax may be levied to dig and wall a well ; as may, also, the *ad valorem* tax, when so voted, specifically. The " hands " may be called out to dig a well, build a fence, open or clear a road, etc.

Relation of the Common School to Other Schools.

1. A Common School is one kept by a teacher having a State or County certificate, or license, for five, or three months, as the law may require, and in which all the children, included in the census, have the privilege of. attending without charge—either direct or indirect.

2. A rate or tuition bill cannot be exacted in a Com· mon School, nor is it lawful to fix any charges, or to *pro rate* the fund on a tuition bill, if thereby any pupil is excluded, or made to pay any sum whatever by any arbitrary, conventional arrangement with the teacher of any private, subscription, or incorporated school. All such arrangements must be voluntary, and embrace nothing coercive.

3. No Common School can be under the auspices of any religious denomination, nor can any religion be taught therein, or any sectarian or infidel tract be read. Under no circumstances can a Common School be attached to, or incorporated with any school belonging to any denomination, no matter how eligible its proposition to do so may seem.

4. A Common School cannot be attached to any University, College, Academy or High School, though under secular control, without the consent of the Commissioner, ratified by a vote of the electors of the District in which it is located, and then only for a period of one year, unless renewed by vote, at the time designated for the election of Common School Trustees. In such cases the Directors, Curators, or other managers become Common School Trustees, charged with the observance of the Rules and Regulations governing Common Schools, and are subject to all the penalties prescribed for ordinary Trustees of Common Schools. No arrangement can be effected with such an Institution which does not accord and render *free* tuition for five months in each year to every common school pupil who pursues the studies prescribed by the Common School laws. If pupils pursue other and higher studies they may be charged for such instruction, and it is not obligatory to *pro rate* the school fund in part payment of such fees. In plain terms, instruction in branches embraced in the Common School course must be taught absolutely free, to every legitimate pupil.

5. Where it does not abridge the rights of pupils, pursuing the elementary studies, prescribed in the Common School course, higher branches may be taught, with the consent of the Trustees, and tuition fees charged for such instruction. The first duty of a Common School teacher is to the pupils pursuing the elementary studies prescribed for the Common Schools.

5. Pay pupils from other districts may be received by the consent of the Trustees, but not in such numbers and studies as will interfere with the proper and thorough instruction of the enrolled pupils of the District.

6. Pupils paying tuition, for any reason, have no rights superior to those attending free. The supreme right to the teacher's best service belongs to the State pupils who attend free, and whose instruction is paid for with the school money apportioned the District.

7. No individual pupil has a personal *pro rata* allotted to him. A given amount of money, upon a census basis, is allotted each district, but the gross amount is for the payment of the teacher, and if a pupil pursues higher or other studies than those pursued in the Common School, he cannot claim, *as a right*, the credit of a *per caput* upon his tuition. The State money is to pay for *a school* in which elementary English studies are taught. In Kentucky *the State* pays nothing for Higher Education. Whenever higher education is given at the public cost, the arrangement is municipal, and not State. High Schools, whereever founded, must be maintained at local expense. The District Tax, provided for in the General Statutes, cannot be applied to the support of High Schools.

8. Whenever and by whatever arrangement of a local character the Common School is taught, the teacher must have a certificate, and the general regulations be observed with regard to the Common School Department.

9. It is the opinion of the Superintendent, that all special acts, giving Institutions the right to receive the Common School Fund, and to *pro rate* the *per capita* upon tuition bills are unconstitutional, and that this has been decided clearly by the Court of Appeals in the case of Halbert *vs.* Sparks, 9 Bush, 259, and of Henderson, Supt., &c. *vs.* R. H. Collins and W. L. Jett, &c., 11th Bush.

School Houses.

1. The Trustees are charged with furnishing a house in which to teach the school. They can not employ a cent or the money apportioned by the State for that purpose.

2. The law provides these ways :

(1.) The voting of an *ad valorem* tax of 25 cents on the $100 (in the county), and 30 cents in the city, for from one to five years.

(2.) The levy of a $2 capitation tax when a majority of the electors consent.

(3.) The calling out of the hands to furnish labor, and implements (as in the case of overseers of roads) for two days in a week until completed.

3. They have a right to secure a site by purchase or a writ of *ad quad damnum*, when the owner of a desired spot will not sell. See " Kentucky School Lawyer," pages 144, 157 of "The Manual of School Architecture," a work that will be furnished any Trustee upon application to the State Superintendent. It contains all that is necessary to know concerning the site, and how to obtain it, the building of the house, containing as it does elevations, plans, and specification forms of contracting, and deeds to the site, the lighting, warming, ventilating and

seating thereof, &c. No house should be built without consulting this book, and a postal-card request to the Superintendent will put the Board in possession of it. We prepared it with great ease, and it contains an exhaustive treatment (illustrated) of the whole subject.

4. The State Boar l has recently given the following important opinion, and we reproduce it as it was published in the original official circular :

SETTLE (PATRON)
     vs.   } Franklin County.
THOMAS B. FORD, C. S. C.

OFFICE SUPERINTENDENT PUBLIC INSTITUTION,

FRANKFORT, KY., September 4th, 1879.

To Commissioners of Common Schools :

1. At a judicial session of the State Board of Education, an appeal was considered from a patron of District No. 36, of Franklin County, from the Commissioner of Common Schools, involving the right of Trustees to levy the $2 capitation tax to complete a school-house, begun under a vote of the District to levy an *ad valorem* tax to build the same. The Commissioner had decided that the will of the majority had been once expressed to support the Trustees in their effort to supply the District with a good house, and that the levy of the capitation tax was legal, the proceeds of the tax on property having proven inadequate. The State Board sustained the Commissioner, or appeal, an abstract of the opinion delivered in behalf of the Board by President Henderson, being as follows, viz : The State contemplates a place in which to carry on the business of education, and requires the Trustees to furnish one. It is clearly implied that the means necessary are to be used when voluntary enterprise is insuffi-

cient to afford the house. The law provides three methods—

1. An *ad valorem* tax, limited, in one year, to 35 cents on the hundred dollars' worth of property.

2. The calling out of the road-hands to work on the house.

3. The levy of a capitation tax.

The only condition, with reference to the tax, is, that the will of the people is to be ascertaine.:. When the people voted an *ad valorem* tax, they said, in effect, we need and want the house. This necessity being apparent, the Trustees, charged with the responsibility to build the house, have the right to exhaust all the means suggested by the law and the reason of the case. They may not levy the $2 poll-tax for the year in which the *ad valorem* tax was levied, because prohibited by a limiting clause in the law. Under the vote in District No. 30, the Trustees began the erection of the house. A decline of values, bankruptcy, etc., decreased the proceeds anticipated from the levy. An unfinished house, unfit for occupancy, was on their hands. They levied the $2 tax to prepare the house for occupancy. Certain parties appealed to the Commissioner ; he sustained the Trustees, and now the case is before the Board, on appeal, for an opinion. The Board, by a majority of its members, gives the following deliverance :

1. When a vote has been taken declaring that a majority favor the erection of a new house, or the repair of an old one, the Trustee may exhaust all the provisions of the law, and, of course, levy the $2 capitation tax. To suppose otherwise, is to assume that the State requires of

them a duty without affording the means by which they may perform it.

2. Where there is *no* house, and the patrons are so indifferent to the education of their children as to be unwilling to vote a tax, or subscribe the money necessary to furnish one, the Trustees may levy the $2 tax, and call out the hands, as many years in succession as may be necessary, to provide a place in which to teach the Common School. The object of the school is not to confer a private benefit, but it is to improve the State's citizenship. The local indifference, therefore, can not stand in the way of the accomplishment of the State'e supreme purpose in education.

3. When a house is supposed to need *repairs*, it requires the favoring expression of the majority before the two-dollar tax can be levied—that is, the District patrons are permitted to express a controlling opinion as to whether the house *needs* repairs.

Under this opinion, Commissioners, acting upon the petition of the Trustees, may order the levy of two dollars in any District in which there is no school-house. They may, after a vote has been taken expressing the necessity of a new house, exhaust all the provisions of the law,

By order of the Board of Education.

HOWARD HENDERSON, President.

Webster's Dictionary.

The State Board of Education has made Webster the standard for Kentucky ; and this action will establish it as the standard of appeal in colleges, academies, and private schools, and with the press, and in literary circles in this Commonwealth. The Board recommends that each school district furnish its school with a copy, regarding it as essential next to an indispensable blackboard. Once purchased, one copy, well taken care of, will last a generation. The latest edition contains nearly 2,000 pages, quarto size, 3,000 illustrations, handsomely engraved, and illustrating, pictorially, every department of natural science, the mechanical arts, mythology, music and musical instruments, history, heraldry.national ensigns, manners, utensils, architecture, fine arts, and costumes of all ages and nations, and will contribute more to convey definite and accurate ideas to pupils' minds than all the printed and oral descriptions that can be given. It also coniains a biographical dictionary, giving the pronunciation of the proper names of nearly 10,000 persons, and much information concerning them. In reading, these persons are being constantly mentioned, and no intelligent progress can be made without knowledge of the characters referred to in the exercise or composition. Who were they? What were they? When did they live? What did they do? are constantly recurring questions; and with an Unabridged at his elbow, the conscientious teacher can always be prepared with an accurate answer. It also defines, spells and pronounces every word, gives its root, derivatives, and its use in polite literature, as sanctioned by the classic writers of the English language, and spoken in the most refined circles of society.

In order to purchase it, the Trustees, after fifteen days' notice, can submit the question to the voters of the district whether they will submit to a levy of $10 (its price) to purchase it ; and that people must be singularly impecunious, or indifferent to the education of its children, when this small sum, to achieve and compass so valuable an end, would be refused. Ten dollars will buy it, and pay all the costs necessary to placing it on the Trustees' desk. When not necessary for contingent expenses, the capitation tax of fifty cents can be used for this purchase, if deemed preferable. Or, in a school of fifty pupils, twenty cents from each child would afford the necessary sum. Any little pleasing entertainment would supply the means of purchase. When purchased, it is the permanent property of the district, and each teacher should be required to receipt for it, and turn it over, at the close of the term, to the Chairman of the Board, taking his

acknowledgment of delivery. So earnestly is the author
of this Manual impressed with the importance of education in the use of our mother tongue—words being the
signs of ideas, conversation being the joy of modern
society, and the power to talk well being one of the
greatest of all accomplishments, and a wide vocabulary
the indispensable to all impressive and effective public
speaking and writing—that he urgently begs each District
Board to give this matter early attention. The Unabridged Dictionary is published by G. & C. Merriam,
Springfield, Massachusetts. The Superintendent has
obtained the special term of $9 a copy to schools at the
place of publication, and $10 a copy when delivered.

Privileges of Teachers.

1. To correct pupils by any method of discipline that
is not cruel. If the rod is used they must not abrade the
skin, whip over the head or neck, or bare feet or legs
If corporal punishment is inflicted in anger, and with
undue severity, it will subject the teacher to a legal prose-
cution. No unusual instrument must be used. If the
ferule is employed, it must not be on the ears, or other
parts where damage (bruises, bone injuries, etc.) might
be done. Pinching, pulling the ears or hair, shutting up
in dark closets, standing pupils upon one leg, suspending
them by the arms, etc., must not be resorted to. Pupils
may be denied recess, and kept in after hours. Extra
tasks should not be imposed.

2. A teacher can suspend a pupil for incorrigible con-
duct, but should immediately report his action to the
Trustees. Expulsion is the province of the District
Board.

3. Teachers have government over pupils on their way
to and from school.

4. Teachers may and should refuse to teach other books
than those prescribed. They may, by the consent of the
Trustees, teach higher branches and charge tuition, but
such instruction must not abridge the rights of Common

School pupils. Teachers may refuse to teach pupils who pursue higher branches than those included in the Common School course.

5. Teachers may legally refuse to teach longer than five months in a term, or six hours a day, except where they have contracted otherwise.

6. Teachers may refuse to adjourn for holidays, and may count the time, though the Trustees may have directed otherwise.

7. Teachers are not required to furnish fuel or perform menial services unless they have so contracted.

8. Teachers do not lose time in consequence of freshets, epidemics, fires and storms, or any other act of God.

9. Teachers may draw 40 per cent of their claims when the school is taught half the time, and 60 per cent when it is completed.

10. Teachers may dispose of their claims in *this way only:* Receipt to the Commissioner for the amount disposed of, and draw an order upon the Commissioner for it in favor of the purchaser.

11. Teachers may require any reasonable and undegrading service of their pupils. They may require cleanliness and neatness.

12. Teachers may, if they choose, read the Bible without note or comment, and have prayers at the opening or closing, but cannot require their pupils, if they or their parents object, to read or join in the prayer. Religious exercises must be absolutely unsectarian.

13. Teachers' wages cannot be garnisheed for debt, but their *tuition fees* can. They are public officers, and the fund apportioned the district is their salary. Their text-books are exempt from execution.

14. Teachers may lawfully resist any order of the Trustees requiring them to adjourn, to surrender the use of the school-house to other purposes.

15. Should Trustees agree that pupils enrolled in an adjacent district may attend the school in their own, the teacher may refuse to teach them, or he may *consent* to do so for or without pay.

16. Teachers may require written reasons for dismissal or forfeiture of certificates, and may appeal from the Trustees to the Commissioner, and from the Commissioner to the State Board of Education.

Duties of Teachers.

1. Must have certificates for *every day* they teach.
2. Must obey strictly the rules and regulations of the State Board.
3. Must teach but one book to a subject to pupils of the same grade.
4. Must keep and return Teachers' Registers as the condition of receiving their last pay.
5. Must attend Institutes on penalty of forfeiting certificates for failure. Can count the time while in attendance, and going and coming.
6. Should use books recommended by the State Board.
7. Must observe the rules prescribed by the District Board, unless they conflict with those of the State Board.
8. Must teach six hours a day, and five months of 22 days each, excluding attendance on Institute and legal holidays. The Institute days and holidays, to be counted, must occur during the school term.
9. Teachers must teach all the children of pupil age in the district, or coming to it by removal of residence, though not included in the census.
10. If assistants are employed to teach in the Common School, they, too, must have certificates ; and if paid by tee Trustees, or with public funds, it is the right of the District Board to employ them.
11. Teachers must contract with a District Board in regular session, and tne majority must concur in their employment.
12. Teachers must have a *programme* and do everything *at the time*, and not allow one recitation to infringe upon the time allotted to another.
13. Teachers are required to work the roads and per.

form militia service as other citizens, and while so engaged they lose the time.

Cautions to Teachers.

1. Teachers are advised *always* to have a written contract with the Trustees, detailing the responsibilities of each, in all particulars not unmistakably defined in the law and rules.

2. Teachers are advised not to sell their claims at a discount, as a promise of the State to pay is the most certain oi all pledges. There may be unavoidable delays, but *never* repudiation.

3. Teachers are advised to remember that they are the commissioned agents of the State; and be careful to follow the prescriptions of the Statutes and the Rules, &c.

4. Teachers are cautioned to avoid all profane and obscene language, to abstain from the use of intoxicating liquors and other vices, as these are legal grounds for removal and the forfeiture of certificates. They should abstain from all exasperating expressions and outbursts of passion in the audience and presence of their pupils.

6. Teachers, while always decorous, should be free from all servility to illegal exactions and unreasoning prejudice and ignorance, and ever bear themselves with dignity and self-respect.

7. Teachers should seek to secure the confidence of patrons and pupils, and to visit them at their homes, as they may have leisure and opportunity.

8. Teachers are cautioned to have a certificate in force at the time of contracting to teach, and for every day they teach. Also, to be present at the organization and during the entire session of the Institute.

9. Teachers, when the Trustees or Commissioner visit the school, are cautioned against complaining in the presence of the pupils, and attempting any dress parade performances to beguile the officers. Regular exercises may be suspended to hear these officers, or to illustrate

particular methods, or the proficiency of pupils, but not for idle chit-chat.

10. Teachers should never use tobacco while teaching, and should be careful of their attitudes, and scrupulously exact in their speech and manners. They instruct or debase as much by *example*, as by teaching orally and professedly.

11. Teachers are advised to insist upon the Trustees furnishing the school-room with necessary aids. Blackboards and a copy of Webster's Unabridged Dictionary are deemed essentials, and no school can be effectively taught without these valuable adjuncts.

Teachers are recommended to provide themselves with such works as "Wilson & Calkins' Object Lessons," Harper Bros., New York; "Phelps' Hand Book," A. S. Barnes & Co., New York and Chicago; "How to Teach," Schermerhorn & Co.;" "Page's Theory and Practice," A. S. Barnes & Co.; "Webster's Academic Dictionary," Ivison, Blakeman, Taylor & Co., New York, and to diligently study the Methods in the Superintendent's Report for 1879.

Life Insurance.

Among the subjects upon which teachers, in common with the educated men of the country, will be held to have some intelligent opinion, is Life Insurance.

Dr. Seiveking commences the introduction to his work entitled "The Medical Advisor in Life Insurance," with the following pertinent remarks :

"Among the features that may be regarded as characteristic of modern society, Life Insurance stands prominently forward as peculiarly unselfish. Its main objcet, provision for those whom death deprives of their bread-winner and protector, entails self-denial and forethought on the part of the individual who takes out a policy, and may thus become indirectly a boon to himself, by compelling thrift, and keeping alive the best feelings of our common humanity. The more the principles of Life In-

surance are understood, the more certain are they to be
appreciated and acted upon : and while they give to society a guarantee of the uprightness and honesty of the
individual, he in return assists in rendering more firm
and stable the very groundwork of the republic. The
relative number of inhabitants of different localities who
have taken out policies of life insurance may not inap-
priately be regarded as an index of the prosperity of the
communities they belong to, for they afford direct evidence of the existence of those qualities, thrift, forethought, and consideration for others, upon which our
social comfort and happiness depend. Those qualities
do not necessarily bear a direct ratio to the amount of
rateable property possessed by those different communities, but they form the practical basis of Christian
society."

The intelligent teacher, who should become a light and
blessing in the community in which he labors, in explo-
ring the varied sources of information with which mind
should be stored, cannot safely omit a subject of so much
importance and interest; and may, at least, so far push
his researches as to enable him to discriminate between
that which rests upon the stable foundations of true
knowledge, from the merely specious and unsound
schemes with which society will always be invaded.

We feel assured that the officers of the Southern Mutual Life Insurance Company of Kentucky, whose ad-
vertisement appears in these pages, will cheerfully direct
the inquirer to the sources of this information. We
commend this institution to the attention of teachers of
Kentucky, as one belonging to the community with whose
interests they are so essentially identified--an institution
of which the late Insurance Commissioner, Gen. Gusta-
vus W. Smith, whose notes on Life Insurance have made
him a leading authority on the subject, has said, "If the
intelligent public men of the State will give a little attention to the subject of Life Insurance, they will find in
the Southern Mutual a home institution, well worthy of
their patronage, and this will result no doubt in estab-

lishing Kentucky Life Insurance on a basis similar to the high financial credit of the State.

Teachers are generally of that class whose remuneration does not enable them to provide otherwise for a dependent family when they may be taken away.

Blank Forms and Instructions.

No. 1.

Certificate of election of Trustee of Public Schools.

To ...., of ...., Greeting :

This certifies that you, the said ...., were at an election held on the .... day of June, Anno Domini 188... chosen to the office of Trustee of Public Schools of......... District, County of ...., State of Kentucky, and you are, by virtue of said election and qualification, fully authorized and empowered to discharge all the duties of said office, and to exercise all the powers thereto belonging according to law, for three years from and including the 1st Saturday in July, 188......

C. S. C.

NOTE.—Forward this to County Commissioner of Common Schools without dely.

No. 2.

Oath of Office.

I do solemnly swear (or affirm) that I will support the Constitution of the United States and the Constitution of the State of Kentucky, and that I will faithfully discharge the duties of Public School Trustee for the ...... School District, in the County of ...., and State of Kentucky, according to the best of my ability. So help me God.

....

Sworn and subscribed to before me, a .... of the

NOTE.—This oath may be administered by any one authorized to administer oaths. Forward without delay to the County Commissioner of Common Schools.

County of .... and State of Kentucky, this ...... day
of ......, Anno Domini 188...

No. 3.

Appointment of Public School Trustees.

In accordance with the power vested in m , I hereby
appoint you, ..., a Public School Trustee for the
...... School District, in the County of ...., and State
of Kentucky, for the term of .... to hold said office until
the next annual election of School Trustees; and you are,
by virtue of this appointment, fully authorized and empowered to discharge all the duties of said office when
you shall have taken the oath of office required by law.

NOTE.—Return this appointment with the oath of office sworn and
subscribed to on the back, to the office of the County Commissioner
of Common Schools.

No. 4.

*Agreement between Public School Trustees and a Pub-
lic School Teacher.*

This agreement, made the .... day of ......, 188......
between ...., party of the first part, and the Board of
Public School Trustees of .....: School District, in the
County of ......, State of Kentucky, parties of the second
part, witnesseth : That the said ...., who holds a legal
certificate, in full force and effect, hereby agrees, for the
consideration hereinafter stated, to teach the public school
in said district for the term of ...., commencing on
the .... day of ...., 188.... ; and further agrees to
enforce the rules and regulations adopted by the State
Board of Education. to adopt the State series of text-
books and the prescribed State course of study, and to
keep the State School Register. as required by law. And
the parties of the second part hereby agree to pay the
said ...., for services duly rendered as teacher of said
school. the sum of ...... dollars, for each and every month
of twenty-two school days, in the manner following, to-
wit : by certifying the school taught half or wholly out
to the County Commissioner for public school money to

58

the credit of said district, or subscription, or local tax as the law prescribes.

In witness whereof, the parties have hereunto set their hands and seals the day and year first above written.
Witness :

[SEAL.]   ....,
                       Teacher.

[SEAL.]   ....,

[SEAL.]   ....,

[SEAL.]   ....,

Trustees of District.

NOTE—It is sufficient that this contract be signed by the Chairman.

No. 5.

Instructions to School Census Taker.

1. Obtain from the Trustees or County Commissioner the exact boundaries of your district.
2. The law requires you to visit each habitation, house, residence, domicile, or other place of abode in your district, and to enumerate the census children of the same by actual observation and interrogation.
3. Report all the statistics to be asked for. Incomplete reports are not to be accepted by the County Commissioner. Do not fail to read the headings of the different columns to be filled in.
4. Include in your report all children (whose parents or guardians are residents of the district) that are absent, attending institutions of learning. Do not include in your report children who are attending institutions of learning or such benevolent institutions as the Deaf and Dumb and Blind Asylums, and Institute for Feeble-minded Children, in your district, but whose parents or guardians do not reside therein.
5. If your district lies partly in two adjoining counties, you must report to the Commissioner of the county in which the school-eouse is located.

6. Be particular that the children listed are properly distributed into columns as headed.

7. Foot up each page. *Check your additions.*

8. You must subscribe to the annexed oath, and deliver, on or before the 10th day of May, a copy of this report to the Chairman of the Board of Trustees.

I do solemnly swear (or affirm) that the facts set forth in the within report are just and true, according to the best of my knowledge and belief, and were collected in strict accordance with law and the instructions given above. So help me God.

....

Chairman of Board of Trustees.

Form of Settlement with Trustees.

A ...... B ...... Chairman of the Board of Trustees, for District No. ...... County of ...., has appeared before me and made satisfactory settlement for all sums arising from local taxation, and this is his quietus, he acting for and in behalf of the Trustees.

C. S. C.

OTHER FORMS.

1. Form for agreement of teachers and Trustees is printed on the cover of the Teachers' Register.

2. Forms for contracting to build or repair a school-house can be found in "Kentucky Manual of School-house Architecture," which can be obtained upon application to the Commissioner or the State Superintendent.

3. For deeds, *ad quod damnun* &c—see forms in "Manual of Architecture," and remarks in "Kentucky School Lawyer" under law, in Art. VII, Chap. 18, Gen'l Stats.

4. The form of oath.

The blanks for Trustee's and Teacher's reports can be found in Teacher's Register.

5. Census blanks, and other papers, such as election notices, poll books, &c., are furnished annually by the Commissioner.

ROBINSON'S SHORTER COURSE

— IN —

ARITHMETIC.

By D. W. FISH, M. A.

———•◆•———

THE SCIENCE OF ARITHMETIC,

Oral (Mental) and *Written*, in all its various grades and
applications, is here treated fully and practically,
in two *comprehensive* and *well graded*
books—Both substantially bound
either in cloth or boards.

The First Book in Arithmetic. An easy and
progressive work, in which oral and written exercises
are thoroughly and practically united. Numerous
illustrations. 168 pp.

The Complete Arithmetic. A comprehensive
Manual on the inductive method, embodying every
form of illustration and exercise, both oral and written. With numerous appropriate designs, and 508
pages.
THE SAME, BOUND IN TWO PARTS.—Designated as Parts I and II.

ECONOMICAL ADVANTAGES.

The "FIRST BOOK," by its natural and systematic develop-
ment and application of numbers, oral and written, is a *full equivalent* of the Table-Book, the Primary, and also for a large part of
the Mental and the Elementary Written Arithmetics of the ordinary series.

The "COMPLETE ARITHMETIC" so thoroughly intro-
duces *mental* arithmetic and the *inductive* method, and so fully
treats all the *higher topics* of the subject, that the use of an Intel-
lectual and Higher Arithmetic would be superfluous; thus a *single
volume* is substituted for an *entire series*.

The *mode of treatment* adopted, not only *logically* trains the
pupil's mind and cultivates his powers of calculation, but will en-
anle both the teacher and the pupil to accomplish far *greater
results* in much *less time* than by the old system.

Hence, it is claimed that a more *thorough system* and *practical
knowledge* of the science of arithmetic can be obtained from these
two books, at *less cost*, and in much *less time*, than from the ordinary series of THREE, FOUR or *more* books.

A positive gain in **money,—time,--labor**, and **superior instruction.**

☞ The Typography and Mechanical finish of all the books of
the series cannot be surpassed.

***KEYS to the above are published for the use of Teachers.

*** *Sample pages and full descriptive circulars will be sent by
mail on application. Liberal term will be made for introduction
and exchange.*

These books substitute Towne's Arithmetics in the list recommended by the State Board of Education.

IVISON, BLAKEMAN, TAYLOR & CO.,

Publishers,

NEW YORK AND CHICAGO.

THE SPENCERIAN
System of Penmanship.

THE COMMON SCHOOL SCERIES. Nos. 1, 2, 3, 4, 4½ and 5. This series has undergone a thorough revision in every particular. Recommended by the State Board of Education.

INTERMEDIATE BOOK. This book contains all the small and capital letters, together with twelve short sentences.

THEORY OF SPENCERIAN PENMANSHIP for schools and private learners. Developed by questions and answers, with practical illustrations.

SPENCERIAN KEY. A standard Text-book on Penmanship, for the use of teachers, pupils and professional penmen. Cloth, illustrated, 176 pages.

SPENCERIAN CHARTS FOR WRITING. 47 Charts; sold separately or bound together. Size, 19 by 24 inches. *Each Capital Letter appears by itself*, with analysis and printed description. The letters are of very large size, the capitals and loop letters being a foot in hight, and the small letters in proportion, so that they may be distinctly seen across the largest school-reem. They are mounted upon rollers in such a manner that one page is exhibited at a time. They are so printed as to present the appearance of **superior blackboard writing.**

⁎ *The Spencerian Copy Books can be had of all booksellers.*
The most liberal terms for introduction will be made.

IVISON, BLAKEMAN, TAYLOR & CO.,

Publishers,

NEW YORK AND CHICAGO.

NICOLAI MARESSHALL,

PORTRAIT PAINTER,

Louisville, Kentucky,

UP STAIRS, CORNER GREEN AND FOURTH.

Has painted portraits of Dr. Henderson and his Wife and Daughter, and gave entire satisfaction.

PORTRAITS PAINTED FROM PHOTOGRAPHS.

OPIUM ANTIDOTE.

B. M. WOOLEY, Atlanta, Georgia,

Has an OPIUM ANTIDOTE that cures this distressing habit, without pain, and by treatment of patients through the mails and the express at their homes. Dr. Henderson, the author of this Manual, was, formerly his preacher in Alabama, and he refers all sufferers to him as to his reliability. It is no substitute for the debasing drug, but a permanent and certain cure for the morbid habit it produces. Let those who are slaves to this tyrant apply to Mr. Wooley, and he will certainly break the despotic chains and set the captive free.

Address him for circulars of information and advice.

A MANUAL

— FOR —

TRUSTEES AND TEACHERS

— OF —

COMMON SCHOOLS.

—BY—

HOWARD HENDERSON,

Late Sup't
Public Instr'n.

COPYRIGHT SECURED.

Bound Copies, with Memorandum Pages attached, can be procured by addressing the Author, and enclosing **40 cts.** The three Trustees and Teachers—4 copies—of any District, will be sent for **50 c'.s. post-paid.**

SINGLE COPIES BY MAIL,   **25 cts.**

"SURE CURE" FOR CATARRH.

HOWARD HENDERSON,

Ex. Supt. Public Inst.

A. T. MITCHELL,

Banker.

We are introducing an *infallible* remedy for **Catarrh, Neuralgic and Nervous Headaches, Colds, Deafness, Dimness of Sight,** and all complaints and complications arising from CATARRH.

It is used as a snuff and contains no hurtful or habit-fixing ingredients.

Relief attends the first applications. It has never failed when taken as directed, and for the maladies it professes to cure. One box lasts a month, and is, in most cases, sufficient to affect recovery of health. So confident are the proprietors of its efficacy, that they will return the money when it fails to effect relief.

"Such men as Elder Ben. Franklin, (deceased), Hons. T. F. Hill, Green R. Kellar and Jas. A. Dawson and Judge Hayes of the Court of Appeals, and Mr. Ed. C. Went, Clerk in the State Superintendents Office, and the Rev. Drs. Milburn, Deems and Miller, and Elders Jacob Creath, J. B. Mayfield, Robert Graham, (Pres't Bible College, Lexington,) and Cols. A. T. Wood, Bruce Champs, and Drs. Weaver, Beck, and thousand others relieved by its use, attest its merits."

—o TERMS: o—

ONE BOX, ONE DOLLAR. THREE BOXES, TWO DOLLARS.

Special Rates to Dealers.

Address:

HENDERSON & MITCHELL,

FRANKFORT, KY.

From Dr. HENDERSON, State Superintendent of Public Instruction, and Mr. A. T. MITCHELL, Banker, of Bourbon County, Ky., are introducing a Catarrh Remedy, discovered by an afflicted friend. Witnesses on the happy effects of their acquaintances, they conferred by chance, and agreed to make its merits known and supply it to sufferers proposing no more at the start, than as philanthrophy. The business grew and pressed them for an adequate supply. While these geutlemen pursue their respective callings as educator and banker, they have competent representatives engaged in the manufacture and sale.

So certain has been the remedy in catarrh and its complications that they have given it "SURE CURE" for a name. Nervous and Neuralgic Headaches, Deafness, Dimness and Dizziness are cured by its use. Many have been relieved of Hay Fever by its use. While these gentlemen could print a hundred testimonials, they trust that their own names are a sufficient guarantee of its worth. Nothing short of a conviction that those who try it will bless their memory could impel them to lend their names to this "CURE."

Circulars with testimonials sent upon application.

One Box for $1.00   Three Boxes for $2.00

Address,

HENDERSON & MITCHELL,
FRANKFORT. KY.

THE SOUTHERN
Mutual Life Insurance Co. of Kentucky,
LOUISVILLE.

OFFICERS:

J. B. TEMPA, President.

A. H. LINDENBERGER, Vice-President.

S. T. WILSON, General Agent.

L. T. THURSTON, Secretary.

JNO. B. SMITH, Treasurer.

D. MERRIWEATHER, JR., Actuary.

The **Insurance Business** of the Company is under the direction of Officers versed in the principles of Life Insurance. It is one of the few Companies in which its mortality experience is computed in its own office every year, with every calculation required in its business.

The **Finances of the Company** are under the control and supervision of a Board of Directors composed of bankers, merchants and lawyers, well known in the community for integrity and ability.

The **Plans** of the Company are those which have been tested by experience and approved by science. All those which have any gambling feature, alluring to such as have not considered, and damaging to the many for the fortunate few, are scrupulously avoided as delusive and improper.

The **Policy** issued by the Company is a clear and plain contract, easily understood by men of ordinary intelligence, and has the following advantages, fully up to the advanced steps of other Companies :

The **rights and obligations** of both parties are clearly stated in the Policy itself.

After **three** annual premiums have been paid, if from any cause **further payment of premiums** is discontinued, the insurance does not thereby cease or become void, but is continued for a definite time, regulated by the number of premiums paid ; or in lieu of this, the policy-holder may elect to take a new paid-up Policy for a definite sum.

Both the **amount** of paid-up Insurance and **time of extension** are stated on each Policy, so that forfeiture for non-payment is prevented and misunderstanding avoided. The Policy cannot be contested except for such gross frauds, of very rare occurrence, which with common regard to the rights of the body of the policy-holders, should prevent payment.

Teachers in Kentucky who can be well recommended, may canvass for the Company during vacation and when other opportunities offer, and earn more than enough to pay for a large policy on their own lives. No license is required, and the study and practice of the principles of Life Insurance will be an agreeable change from the routine of the school-room. For information apply to the Officers of the Company.